LATEST BEST GUIDE TO PURSUING WEALTH

Chinedu Aneke

DISCLAIMER

The purpose of this ebook is to educate and the author and the publisher shall neither liability nor responsible to per-person or entity with respect to any loss or damage caused or alleged to be caused directly or indirectly by this book.

DEDICATION

I personally dedicate this book to you who is reading this, I took out time energy and few resources to make sure that you get access to this book manual so that you can read it, learn the most important things that you really needs to know that will help you greatly. I also dedicate this manual book to all my well wishers, those who are willing and ready to support me for my next book, I thank you all, I mostly thank you for buying this book, it's a way of supporting me to be able to continue to write more for you to learn.

ACKNOWLEDGEMENT

Firstly, I acknowledge and thank the Almighty GOD for the wisdom, His love and mercy towards me. Gratitude goes you who reads this, also to those who believe in me, those who supported me, both family and friends, I appreciate and thank you all.

CONTENTS

	Acknowledgments	Pg4
	Introduction	Pg6
1	Chapter 1	Pg7
	Principles to unlock wealth	Pg7
	Five principles to unlocking wealth	Pg7
2	Chapter 2	Pg16
	Steps to personal wealth	Pg16
	Achieving your goals	Pg17
	The keys to succes	Pg18
3	Chapter 3	Pg29
	The inevitable mistakes	Pg29
	The law of success	Pg30
4	Chapter 4	Pg36
	Understanding failure	Pg36
	Paving your path to success	Pg39
	The law of prosperity	Pg41
	Affirmation to fulfilment	Pg45
	Conclusion	Pg48

INTRODUCTION

Among many factors, one of the maximum tough factors to reconcile in existence is the anomaly that struggling exists on this global. Suffering is eminent. Of direction, what's similarly critical is knowing that the purchase and ownership of wealth isn't always a ruler that measures one's happiness. If pleasure honestly had been to be located in materials, then all people who enjoy the 'thrill' of it through entering touch with the item might examine the identical degree of pleasure. In lifestyles, guys are constantly stimulated with the aid of using inevitable impulses of repulsion – from sorrow and yearning to looking for pleasure and absolute fulfillment. In the search to embody all happiness, he's pressured to run after the exciting and agreeable, whilst confronting the opposites, he avoids unwanted gadgets and unpleasant environments.

CHAPTER 1

Principles to unlock wealth

Honestly, the truth is this, at some point of history, all achievers aware or subconsciously have used 5 concepts, that are not unusualplace to absolute development in all factors of lifestyles.

The five Principles to Unlocking Wealth:
These ideas are a key to unlocking splendid cache of wealth, abundance and fulfillment. They are all targeted on our real innate traits, which as a count of truth are conventional and feature a religious basis. These standards are:

a. Truth
b. Righteousness
c. Peace
d. Love, and
e. Non-violence

The exercise of those virtues will allow everybody to development in lifestyles with none doubt.
The purpose is easy.
These usual concepts are all appealing and unnecessary to say, they shape the cornerstones of the code of ethics. You can't pass incorrect working towards the significance to ethical values, codes of behavior and obeying the Law of Nature for your pursuit of Wealth. In the approaching pages, you'll find out the intention of attaining monetary freedom even as on the identical time, obtaining the proper artwork of happiness via the information that the degree of pleasure isn't 'immediately' proportional to simply financial wealth.

This concise, specific and straight-to-the-factor manuscript explores avenues which can be maximum genuinely going to extrade your existence for the better. Unlike many different books at the equal situation, this manuscript delves on difficulty regions applicable to factors of your private lifestyles and increase that I can assure will deliver again that smile in your face. It is clear, centered and exceptionally a readable e book, which you'll revel in.

While pessimism warns us of risks lurking earlier than our very very own eyes, optimism may also propel us into fake security.
Pessimism must most effective be taken into consideration preliminary and now no longer a very last catch 22 situation in any state of affairs – that is step one to fulfillment.
Time and again, we had been subjected to times which might be disturbing, and deep inside us we 'understand' the capacity risks and dangers surrounding us, and the 'voice' inside adamantly rejects this threatening state of affairs confronting us, as such due to the fact we fail to apprehend this 'voice' inside us our intellectual clinging to the outer international detaches us from the internal voice of 'TRUTH' thereby throwing us absolutely of the tracks because it had been.
The 2nd step to achievement and wealth is to persuade your self of the significance of self-control, self attention and self-field.
We need to pay attention to the voice inside and recognize the lifestyles of the innate pressure or the Dynamic Willpower – the effective energy expressing thru the thoughts, frame and the mind! Thus the second one step qualifies which you broaden religion in now no longer simply what you may do and acquire however most significantly growing religion in your self (your innate, inherent and latent characteristics).
Step 3 calls for that via steady vigilance, using the energy of intelligence, self evaluation and introspection and via cautious information and use of those concepts, you could learn how to stay past the needs of the thoughts in something surroundings you discover your self – this can qualify you to put in force and include the street to wealth.
There isn't anyt any such factor as a unfastened lunch. If you hate to install any paintings/attempt however like to achieve fulfillment, you'll must rethink your views.
So to gain the latter, you need to do the previous and the realistic concept is to discover what absolutely offers us pride after which discover if it's miles feasible to make cash from doing it.
"If you don't begin you'll not be triumphant."

Pursuing Wealth

The statement 'haste makes waste' stands authentic even nowadays, and extra frequently than now no longer, a number of us have a tendency to sense annoyed while we can't stay as much as our beliefs and the requirements we set for ourselves all of the time. On different occasions, we may also experience that had we taken the undertaking that got here our manner that possibly matters may also nicely have modified for the better, but there may be additionally the opportunity that during our over tension to attain the intention we strive too tough and burn ourselves out absolutely!

The query that now stays to be requested how will we start, how are we able to obtain achievement in lifestyles?
Well, my friend, relaxation confident that this ee-e book has been written to reply this query satisfactorily, casting off confusion or anomalies whatsoever. There are many techniques that you can still rent and diverse way via which you could plough your self to attaining the intention. One not unusualplace thread in they all is self-belief, self-righteousness or honesty and moral living (in words, deeds, mind and actions) pertaining in your lifestyle – that is Step four. In any enterprise the emphasis on ethical and moral requirements ranks the highest, and this must now no longer be neglected or overlooked. The most effective manner to reap equanimity, stability or equilibrium even once you emerge as the wealthiest person is to have your experience of figuring out the actual essence of lifestyles. Nothing in existence is consistent. Life is ever converting and matters that appear to have lifestyles nowadays might also additionally end to exist the next day and that is a truth which you – and every person else – ought to learn how to accept.

Step 5, while you find out some thing profound and beautiful, the herbal tendency is to percentage it with others. In the subsequent chapters what you may find out are the real approaches to gain entire fulfillment, and that is a ee-e book as a way to will let you unharness your innate characteristics to the fore, thereby permitting

you to achieve the advantages and the rewards that heaps of humans everywhere in the global at this very 2nd are playing due to the fact they have got turn out to be rich. Following the manual in the coming pages, and it's miles my honest accept as true with that everyone has the capacity to achieve existence.
"Wealth is greater than simply cash."

The Ladder to Success

It is the privilege of guy to attain all spherical greatness, and in fact fulfillment must be one's habit. Man is basically perfect, and consequently limitless are the opportunities that lie dormant in him. In order to convey out the very fine from inside, a lifestyles prepared and flawlessly disciplined for the invention of the possibilities that lie lurking inside us, is a lifestyles nicely spent. The crucial factor isn't always what number of abilities every on people has, however the significance need to be centered on how a whole lot of our present abilities, attributes and talents are we organized to expand, exploit, discover and put into effect in our every day lives. The query you ought to ask, is whether or not you're making a realistic use of at the least one high-quality expertise mendacity inherent inside you? The one ideally suited essential essential is to recognize that every one our fulfillment absolutely relies upon upon ourselves.

The fine manner to be satisfied is to do the matters which you evidently love and revel in doing – some thing which you are surely passionate about! Likewise the pleasant manner to be triumphant and come to be rich is to look to it which you reap the matters you've got got earnestly preferred to are seeking in lifestyles. This would require which you put into effect your efforts in to sports with a purpose to permit you to degree fulfillment. For example the easy manner to give an explanation for that is to think about the subsequent instance: in case you take a liking for artwork, painting, and drawing then the manner to continue is to searching for steerage on approaches to go into competitions, and approaches to put up your paintings through galleries (technique galleries without delay and go away paintings on a sale or go back basis) or exceptional artwork publishers' or maybe exposing your expertise through getting into seasonal gala's wherein you may discover a big collecting of all sorts of retailers.

You might also additionally need to feature diverse distinctive forms of subject matters for your artwork portfolio with a view to maximize your talents to attain an target target market some distance and huge with pastimes in exclusive subject matters/subjects.
Contact groups, boards or even Internet newsgroups and discover diverse different avenues (including photographers, image and framing galleries, arts councils and authorities groups that offer assist consisting of loans etc.) in an effort to let you step up your enquiry – the concept is to pursue the aim relentlessly and with a advantageous mind-set. As some distance as your theme/concern be counted is involved submit questions, polls, surveys, and determines what humans are searching for, after which genuinely discover the want and fill it. Every little will assist, however it's far the pressure required to get the momentum going and this is the important thing factor. Another beneficial factor isn't to simply try, attempt to to maintain trying – as an alternative expand an mindset wherein you DO the factor you've got got determined to pursue, put into effect and practice the techniques proven on this ee-e book. Finally do now no longer simply prevent at that – preserve religion and do now no longer yield to any defeat.

Once you've got got determined to place the 'plan' into action, make certain that it's far stored ignited and glowing…rejections and disappointments need to in no manner curtail your hope, development and your choice to fulfillment. People who've succeeded regardless of all of the hardship, ache and conflict have stimulated endless tens of thousands and thousands across the global – it's time you too set an instance for others to observe on your footsteps. You need to consider that the strategies hired through special people in buying wealth can be distinct, however the intention is not unusualplace to all, and the stairs spoken of in advance are in impact your equipment in your average fulfillment. Very robust self-control is wanted so that you can expand internally, and the want for 2 maximum critical attributes, specifically braveness and self belief are critical ingredients. Thus poverty and prosperity does now no longer always rely on understanding wholly (e.g. enterprise acumen, advertising techniques and so on) however it surely relies upon at the 3 C's and they're character, creativity and your innate abilities.

Courage and self belief by myself can result in precise transformation at the same time as the other will handiest convey an awful lot sorrow and depression in instances of misery and crisis. However, regardless of existence's issues we ought to face up to barriers and obstacles and as such continuously remind ourselves of the ideally suited inherent or innate strength which all of us posses and which we will all correctly expand thru non secular insight. Thus ignoring our talents and capacity for growing the private energy that we want for going via ego- breaking studies calls for gigantic fortitude and field, and I give an explanation for to you on this ee-e book on how you can acquire all this right here and now. Without those features you're destined to fail, and this is the cause why a massive part of humans experience despondent due to the fact they were given into opposition or they absolutely gave up beneathneath pressure, thru loss of self-braveness and dynamic strength of mind. When our fantasies and expectancies aren't fulfilled, there's a bent for us to revert to our antique methods – the hollowness we revel in may be maximum stressful and we can't forget about it forever. A lot of the time what precisely occurs is that something suitable we adopt in lifestyles, it does now no longer suggest we can keep.

This isn't always due to the fact an not possible field is needed however due to the fact we lack braveness and self assurance we're beaten with bad mind-set – that is what stops the entirety in its tracks! The preliminary burst of enthusiasm starts to fade, and what regarded so top notch will become a peril a catch 22 situation and a problem. The thoughts takes over and questions surmount elevating doubts after doubts whether or not the complete concept or idea is worthwhile – a warfare ensues, the thoughts says the only element and the mind and our instinct urges us to comply with the course to 'fulfillment'. Even earlier than we start the adventure the cease is imminent, due to the fact we're not sure what genuine course to observe. Success lies in what you're making of it now no longer what you 'think' it need to be (do now no longer fantasize fulfillment).

Formula to Success

What you observed and the way then you definitely act is the determining element to help you find out the aim of fulfillment. These attributes are critical collectively with a hard and fast of constant ideas, that you comply with thru. Thoughts primarily based totally on purpose are a effective catalyst to begin any reaction, and after you set off, you may quickly recognize that braveness is the easy distinctive feature wanted for a person to traverse the rocky road. Obstacles are herbal, and they're a way to the supply of obtaining wealth, as I am positive you may agree. Persistence, persistence and perseverance will need to be practiced religiously to attain the intention and to triumph over the barriers. Of route that said, I might now want to factor out the P's which you ought to frown upon. Do now no longer procrastinate, do now no longer fake which you realize it all and eventually do now no longer extend your 'venture(s)'. Be organized to combat the hindrances which could confront you, however pursue your aim and permit your capacity self-discipline to predominate.

In any scenario in lifestyles, it's far unequivocally vital to stay degree headed, in spite of all of the 'ups and the downs' that we're possibly to face. Remember existence is dualistic with the aid of using nature – the obverse and the opposite aspects of the identical coin to place it truely. I am forced to feature that aleven though we realize that the beyond is the purpose and the existing is the impact.

There is a completely deep that means embroiled on this syntax, and if you may relate this to achievement, then it could be stated that if we intelligently stay withinside the clinical self-area, we will turn out to be the architects of our personal destiny.

The Basic Steps

The following suggestions will assist you pave a high-quality route in your closing fulfillment.
The steps are quite simple to enforce on your day by day existence.

1. Do what you like and what you're accurate at.
2. Be organized to analyze and to be fine (motivation and enthusiasm).
3. Be an revolutionary person.
4. Be organized to make investments now no longer simply cash however a while, attempt and resources, too.
I stated cash – this doesn't imply that you need to make investments a big sum to turn out to be a millionaire or wealthy.
5. You ought to be disciplined in having set dreams and targets. Remember that endurance is the important thing to achievement.
6. You ought to be organized to control a while correctly.
7. As you evolve, learn how to deliver lower back what you amass to the society. I name this philanthropy.

You have to have a strong vision – one in that you 'see' your self having attained achievement. Great humans of the beyond and gift see to it that they attain this coveted position, through using those simple steps. However, be aware in step 2 I intentionally used the phrase 'analyze', and that too for a superb motive. Life is the best teacher, for that reason you have to be inclined to just accept demanding situations all of the time (the use of the strength of discrimination) and accordingly as a end result you have to study through its everlasting concepts the remarkable doctrine it has found out with the passing of time. This method which you should act whilst the time is proper. Action is exceedingly vital and highlights achievement – the 2 are synonymous to be pretty sincere. To prevail motion is wanted however the crucial element is how severe you're. Being too critical can destroy your commercial enterprise challenge, so the factor is to have FUN.

Any field would require agency and orderliness. You ought to as I stated withinside the creation be organized to pay attention on your internal voice as lots as you likely can. This manner that in preference to being too depending on your family, pals and so on (now no longer that that is horrific) start to believe for your personal capabilities. Stand-by myself and attempt to analyze and prevail. Often, screw ups may also simply end result from times wherein we've stopped exercise our very own perspectives, or we've emerge as too depending on others'. Success isn't always a few mystery that you need to look for or unearth on the way to attain your destination; it's miles instead the knowledge or the popularity aspect which you broaden with appreciate to what you actually need in existence. Intuition, braveness, skills, expertise, demanding situations and possibilities are a number of the principles that decide the developments of those who revel in wealth. Any undertaking done with the proper spirit will come up with victory. Mental mindset is what is going to come up with fulfillment, however terrible mind-set, laziness and running unwillingly will bring about failure. Do not count on an excessive amount of in too brief a time, however your method ought to be tremendous and execute your undertaking with absolute perfection, paying specific interest on your long-time period aim(s). This way which you technique your responsibility with focused electricity and also you execute your plans righteously. This must be your philosophy of lifestyles.

To start a brand new assignment, it vitally critical which you understand the following, which I actually have to mention is crucial. You need to admire the truth that to begin a commercial enterprise you want to acquaint your self with the time period coins flow. Investment withinside the shape of a capital is a requirement, however greater importantly it's far the idea of viability of the commercial enterprise mission that topics maximum.

CHAPTER 2
Steps to Personal Wealth

Decision-making is possibly the toughest step to recover from with to your quest to start the adventure to wealth. The trouble is till you do now no longer delve deep inside your self to free up your innate characteristics possibilities are that you'll be indecisive and hesitant. This isn't always incorrect as such, however extra regularly than now no longer this 'feeling' might not permit you to maximize your complete ability. There isn't anyt any mystery to unleashing your complete-blown ability – the 'mystery' lies on your willingness to pay attention in your internal voice. The initiative to capture an awesome possibility that comes your manner is through project the project in a methodical manner. Sit quietly, calm your senses and mind, and meditate deeply at the challenge depend in query. Do now no longer leap into something right now simply due to the fact the concept appears favorable. Most matters seem very 'accurate' withinside the preliminary phase, however questioning, making plans and time are a prerequisite. Often it's far some thing inside so that it will inform you what to do.

The mystery isn't always from with out, however may be received from inside. Striving to do your very pleasant always is the little mystery to help you amass wealth. Imagination (I suggest optimistic creativeness) that is the electricity to visualise is an critical component in innovative idea – however as you'll admire you'll now no longer be capable of do that with out a sturdy will, and specifically this college of visualization must be ripened into company perception and conviction.

1. You have to have the preference to gain your aim of fame – that is rule variety one.
2. Be organized to address cash efficaciously with appreciate to budget, expenditure and obligation and/or accountability.
3. Do now no longer spend extra than you're required to and spend much less than you make.
4. Personal troubles, along with dependancy now no longer simplest

to pills etc., may be ruinous. This is some thing that need to be sorted from the very onset.

5. Figure out approaches to make investments and primarily start to store cash. You will need to play clever and get your priorities genuinely proper.

In any task, it's miles in all likelihood that you can face lots of antagonism, a much cry from an idealistic state of affairs. Over expectations, over optimism and the tendency to 'desire' that matters run as planned, can and frequently may also result in failure. Thus as noted in advance making plans may be very vital on your achievement. Of direction the opposite elements that one desires to bear in mind are also over paintings and exhaustion. In the desire to make your millions, the opportunity is which you becomes a pissed off ruin and end up pretty despondent – this can now no longer be beneficial to your development or pursuit to wealth.

Achieving Your Goal

When you persevere refusing to simply accept failure, realize that the item you've got got got down to attain will materialize via the dynamic willpower. Thoughts may be tremendously effective tools, and in case you are inclined to put in force this divine present you then definately are positive to acquire your purpose. If you hang to a positive idea with dynamic willpower, it assumes a tangible outward shape. Now is the time to cauterize the bad traits inherent withinside the shape of habits, loss of sturdy willpower, loss of self belief, hesitance and incorrect mindset toward lifestyles in popular. You have inside you the strength to perform the entirety you need, that energy lies withinside the will.

The root reason of failure in existence is loss of awareness – do now no longer hoard your self with thoughts, principles and techniques all of sudden withinside the very wish to be triumphant. Begin slowly and be steady for your aim placing scheme. Focus your interest on one element at a time, and do now no longer permit your mind to head in a country of 'over drive'. There is a systematic manner of using attention, and the magic phrase is to maintain calm, whilst you carry out all of your obligations with the right speed. Never rush and create chaos, however alternatively methodically and meticulously consciousness and centre your complete thoughts on anything you adopt, and the vital aspect is to hold your thoughts flexible. Once which you are clearly at the proper tracks and at the route to accomplishing your aim, do exercising care as a ways as time control is concerned. It is regularly very smooth to get concerned with a mission a lot so you can get over excited in perfecting some thing it's far which you are doing.

You ought to prioritize your paintings and especially appreciate and honor the price of time – do now no longer waste it slow and your existence!

The Keys to Success

As I actually have cited the surroundings performs a big position as it's far pretty inevitable – specifically our internal surroundings.

A calm comfortable person is a long way much more likely to pop out a winner in a attempting state of affairs than his/her counterpart – someone who his apprehensive annoyed and erratic. The former has his senses completely recognized with the surroundings wherein he locations himself. However, the stressed person does now no longer recognize the surroundings and therefore receives into hassle. The key phrases are consciousness, attention and care in something you do in existence.

1. Develop a particular and a straight forward aim/purpose.
2. Draw up a smart possible plan/program.
3. Guard your fitness. Without fitness there's no actual wealth.
4. You have to preserve your strength.
5. Be sincere on your lifestyles (in phrases, deeds, mind and movements).
6. Stick to virtues and undertake precise ideas.
7. Reflect upon best personalities and are trying to find energy from their philosophy.
8. Seek divine steerage and be trustworthy.
9. Endeavor to assist and serve others with gratitude.
10. Always suppose high-quality and accept as true with withinside the energy of God.

Transformative wondering is certainly the manner to fulfillment. Set out a plan to gain your intention and intentionally ruminate over the that means of this plan and make it happen.

From time immemorial first rate human beings from all walks of lifestyles have emerged as genuine victors and the purpose at the back of that is education the thoughts for happiness. Ethical subject is critical, especially self-field. Each person is unique. What is ideal for individual A might not be appropriate for individual B. However, it needs to be emphasised that every one can experience quietude, solitude and silence, and to be sincere each person no matter age, caste, creed, color, intercourse has at a few degree or some other skilled peace. After coming across via trial and blunders method, you could decide the suitable manner to compose your thoughts frame complicated and accordingly achieve remarkable heights. Meditation might not be powerful for all, however that doesn't imply which you do now no longer improvise such techniques as and while required. Be systematic, and your simplest aim ought to be to rent techniques that carry you achievement and happiness.

Our intellectual colleges decide our movements, and it's miles pretty apparent that the thoughts need to be tamed and subdued. Constant vigilance is important and non-stop education of the thoughts will pave the direction to closing fulfillment. Never fall prey to the dictates of your thoughts! Optimistic, heroic and noble beliefs have a effective and uplifting impact upon the frame. Enthusiasm with planned nicely-orchestrated self-utility in joyous temper and absolute optimism is the name of the game direction to wealth for all high-quality men.

The Power of Thoughts

The previous bankruptcy highlighted the significance of cultivating accurate mindset and growing religion in what you are searching for to obtain in existence. Nothing in existence is impossible, except you suspect it so. Thoughts are remarkable 'packets' of electricity and in case you tenaciously hang to a sure concept with the dynamic willpower, there may be no cause why this idea can not take place consistent with the blueprint you've got got created. Earlier I in brief stated via way of means of explaining how someone inquisitive about artwork can step up his or her competencies to excel in lifestyles. I shall now use the identical instance to demonstrate the strength of concept. An artist develops an concept of making a portray or a drawing of a stunning landscape. The notion manner initiates a sequence of thoughts and the artist sooner or later makes use of those thoughts to provide the skeleton paintings, which lets in him/her to finally entire the very last paintings of artwork in step with the intellectual blueprint created initially. A mere concept method permits the artist to create the masterpiece!

This advent is in itself a systematic major primarily based totally at the Universal Law Of Creation. It is the supply from which the entirety manifests. It is in us all, and it could definitely be tapped in case you are simply inclined to offer it a move. The mystery isn't always honestly a mystery, however it's miles a treasure trove inside every and each one folks and we've the proper to apply it maximum efficaciously. Is it now no longer proper that whilst you see a person so very satisfied and elated, your thoughts receives stuck up with the cheer and also you find out that there's a grin in your face?

The mind are so carefully interweaved with the thoughts. If the mind are calm the thoughts is calm. In any issue of lifestyles, be it beginning a enterprise, getting your first task or getting married, the connection of thoughts and concept is most important. Systematically, consequently we should teach and field the thoughts for proper questioning and diligent activity, and therefore have accurate information of what you really need in lifestyles, and the way this could upload to the helpful dynamism on your quest and what you in the long run are looking for – your course to achievement and wealth becomes gracious, significant and attainable! People with sure characteristics are nearly magnetically attracted, and such characteristics are referred to as tremendous characteristics.

These traits are found in all folks, however they're now no longer invoked or sincerely understood. We recognise what love, kindness, braveness and pleasure imply, those are noble virtues, and we additionally understand them as characteristics we recognize in others. Despite understanding this, whilst we act we act compromising beliefs. The cause at the back of that is that we're in no way actual to our personal selves – we're continuously appearing and placing up a 'show' to delight all and sundry round us, however ourselves! It is painful, demoralizing and pretty agonizing now no longer to be your authentic self. You may also exclaim in disbelief, and sat what has this were given to do with wealth and prosperity? I well known your concern, however I humbly request which you take a second or , and withinside the silence of the night time ruminate over this factor deeply. I would really like then you to put into effect what I stated above via way of means of being your self.

Notice the adjustments that arise with the passage of time, and what you'll really find out is that once you can actually convey out into expression the perfume of one's innate effective characteristics or traits (of who you surely are), then not most effective humans however all of the matters which you have ever preferred or needed for will come to you. "As the idea, so the thoughts."

In order to satisfy your set dreams and your dreams, it's far important to exercise what the ee-e book outlines. The recurring inclination of our concept styles is in the long run the determining component, which determines our talents, abilities and our non-public traits.

Based in this vital and essential piece of expertise, one assumes that the ones fortunate few had been born with the unique expertise you lack and fervently preference to have.

To a big quantity that is real, however it needs to be stated that nobody is born a millionaire – complete prevent! The precious statistics lies withinside the artwork of cultivating the sample that brings achievement. We are what we assume we're.

It is authentic whilst Masters say that, "Your Thoughts create the surroundings".

- Thoughts expand persona
- Thoughts sell fitness
- Thoughts affect the frame
- Thoughts can extrade and form the destiny (destiny)
- Thoughts bring on introduction
- Thoughts affect the body structure and psychology of humans
- Thoughts can convey achievement
- Thoughts may even heal the frame

Watch your mind continuously. Your stories and the surroundings have their 'seat' in mind.

Your idea, and autosuggestions through meditation and visualization strategies have to be more potent than the 'mind, and whilst your movements uplift you, understand which you have

understood the artwork of controlling your idea processes.
You can accomplish something thru the strength of idea.
Visualization makes use of your creativeness to permit your self to 'picture' your fulfillment or reaching your earnest aim.
Your intellectual mind or vibrations are relatively effective, due to the fact the thoughts has a tangible reference to your mind and your moves. Your mind are diffused energies and feature a robust connection to our consciousness.
Therefore, consistent nourishment of fine mind through visualization, yoga and meditation will carry harmony, happiness, fitness and wealth!

Factors That Bring Inertia

First and principal is to introspect, and this actually way which you take inventory of your trends and habits. Often, loss of self-evaluation is the reason of our brief fall, and it's miles the shortage of particular, undivided attempt and interest that stands for your manner to development and success of your preferred purpose. Introspection consequently way reassessment of our intellectual 'block' and diagnosing deficiencies through removing bad inclinations withinside the shape of habits, indecisiveness, worry, loss of self belief and so on – what we frequently time period as screw ups. It is time to reenergize in order that through uprooting these kinds of negativities out of your lifestyles the real happiness with the keenness to development will become distinguished and firmly rooted.

The best enemy that prevents us from advancing in existence apart from apathy, loss of self assurance and inferiority complicated is fear. Fear will actually prevent us from transferring forward – in truth we are able to now no longer even satisfy our very purpose to be triumphant. The excellent manner to fight worry is to exercise deep respiration exercises, and each night time mentally verify which you are beneathneath the safety of the superb character of godhead, and energize your mind with advantageous feelings. Consciously uproot the seeds of worry from inside through forceful awareness upon braveness, and shift your consciousness to a degree that lets in you to absolutely recognize which you are past any kind or form of hurting. Fear comes from the coronary heart, so fill your coronary heart with LOVE, and whilst you sense agitated relax, chill out and breathe rhythmically, enjoyable with every exhalation.

Of route there's but any other hassle, which I accept as true with, is the most important purpose of frustration and ultimately dampening our capacity to excel in existence. It is, what I name 'desirous of outcomes with out the desire to place withinside the attempt'. I even have for my part failed due to this kind of terrible outlook – and I am the primary one to confess this openly. Now that is in which the factor I made above will become clearer. Failure, sorrow, infection and inadequacies are herbal scenarios whilst the Law of Nature is broken. Transgression and violation of the everlasting Law of nature brings misery. As people we've the competencies to form, accurate and extrade our lives, dreams and destiny. The finest obstacle that you may ever meet on your lifestyles is your on the spot surroundings. If some thing you may ought to alternate that – you could have observed that I began out this ee-e book sounding barely cynical and fairly over careful, a whole lot much less a touch bad – the high cause for this can now turn out to be apparent.

The surroundings that I simply stated may be described into , specifically the internal and the outer. It is those fields of surroundings that you'll need to be careful for. All your studies come out of your thoughts stuff – or the internal surroundings (mind). What you understand thru all of your senses from the out of doors will similarly form your destiny. Thus the essential factor right here is to preserve watch over your mind. My inspiration to you is to watch out for your internal surroundings extra so than your outer surroundings. For instance you could have stumbled upon a brilliant domestic enterprise possibility this is probably incredible and simply proper for you in each issue.

You are satisfied, and pretty inclined to provide it a pass...but on reflection some thing approximately this enterprise 'stops' you from going in advance with it. There can be numerous motives for this, however I am very curious to analyze the foremost cause. Rest confident it can't be the cash (due to the fact it's far inside your budget), nor can it's a hype (as it has reputedly labored for hundreds with testimonials to confirm). So what's it I wonder? Think approximately this factor, and you'll absolute confidence come to a positive conclusion...and exceptionally it's far, the thoughts stuff – the perpetrator. To achieve lifestyles you'll need to start with the aid of using correcting your notion styles, due to the fact it's far the employer of your mind and the affinity you've got got for them in an effort to decide your fate.

"Thoughts explicit thru the bodily frame."

The Risk Factor

Without digressing from the situation count number, I would really like to remind you what I noted withinside the early levels of the ee-e book concerning the dualistic nature of lifestyles.

Why is it that a few humans are so fortunate and but others fall at the back of withinside the battle to be triumphant? To solution this conclusively it's miles really well worth noting that during popular majority of humans have the belief that prosperous human beings have some thing unique which they glaringly lack – This isn't authentic as all of us recognize, but what makes one individual richer than the opposite is essentially dependant on the selection or the choice taken, coupled with the hazard(s) stated thru the more information of the energy of discrimination, and the cappotential to weigh and stability the scales of your intuitive school. Now the danger which you take has were given to be one primarily based totally at the know-how that the challenge you've got got determined to pursue has been researched thoroughly.

You most effective embark upon taking a using check as an instance when you sense which you are gifted sufficient to byskip it and now no longer otherwise. Thus, the hazard which you adopt on this regard has were given to be what I name an knowledgeable hazard. In different phrases, it's miles one in which you've got got self belief on what you are becoming your self into, and this too is primarily based totally on records supply which you have searched nicely. The reality which you at the moment are studying this record is to benefit the knowledge on a way to gain economic achievement – accordingly this record is in a manner your studies device to allow you to then put into effect the strategies and the pointers mentioned to attain the purpose. The motion taken has consequently come immediately from a supply that may be taken into consideration authentic, treasured and genuine. Once you sense assured to take the riding take a look at with the steerage of the using teacher of direction, you make a decision to take the riding check – that is the precise manner to make sure achievement. I desire to redress a factor made formerly and it's miles approximately getting to know. You should be inclined to research continuously, due to the fact to advantage any skill, know-how and electricity, you ought to be organized to learn. Commitment is the essential pressure that you have to very a lot get used to from the very onset. Remember that there are sure conditions that you can not have direct manage to convey any foreseeable modifications, which can also additionally bring about a great deal heartache. However, this want now no longer ever be the case due to the fact what genuinely subjects is the mechanism or the way in that you manage the state of affairs and in the long run how nicely you react to it. The problem with us is that we have a tendency to stay withinside the beyond and withinside the destiny on the equal time. When our intellectual school will become over stressed we turn out to be discouraged.

The load is simply too heavy for the thoughts, so we ought to limition the load. When we've an excessive amount of to do at one time, we must without delay prevent our activities. The clock ticks on at a normal pace, it can not tick twenty 4 hours away in 60 seconds, nor are you able to do in a single hour what you could do maximum efficaciously in twenty 4 hours. Live for the now, and the 'destiny' will contend with itself. Do not be grasping and particularly do now no longer burn your self out via way of means of 'wanting' to grow to be a millionaire! The tables have became round, increasingly more humans are resorting to a easy lower back to fundamentals lifestyle – with out such a lot of luxuries and less issues.

The dualistic idea of nature is everyday everywhere – you can't prosper in case you write out cheques while not having credible price range or credit (deposit) for your financial institution account, eventually you'll run out of cash. Without peace of thoughts, the possibly hood of strolling out of 'steam', happiness, calmness and power you becomes 'bankrupt' mentally, emotionally, spiritually and bodily drained. What a pity it'll have all been to return back to some

extent of utter desolation!
This is whilst you need to live at the energy inside, and mentally verify your reason in lifestyles; you could need to undergo a few great enjoy so you neglect about your concerns completely. The factor is do now no longer take something too seriously, experience what you've got got and be glad with what's your due.

What You Must Avoid
It is herbal that once the unexpected takes place we're some distance much more likely to react in a bad manner. However this want now no longer be so, the ee-e book famous methods to attain your intention harmoniously and diligently.
The following are a few guidelines so as to be maximum beneficial:
1. When matters move incorrect do now no longer overreact. Think definitely and calmly.
2. Never be over judgmental, and over essential.
3. Try now no longer to disregard a terrible state of affairs, watch out for the consolation zone.
4. Wisdom and electricity on my own allow you to triumph over an awful lot of lifestyles's approaching issues.
5. Tackle issues head on.
6. Avoid greed and vanity of any kind.
There is a enterprise ethics and a businessman have to exercise this ethics. Those who're strictly sincere and honest will flourish in enterprise. Let us once more don't forget artwork as an instance to focus on what has been mentioned for this reason some distance. As all of us realize we've got innate powers – inside every and anyone folks lies the storehouse of latent electricity bursting to be 'awakened'.
Let us expect which you have the innovative energy, and that being an artist for instance you could absolutely paint and draw any difficulty or theme.
Fair sufficient, it's far apparent which you have vast expertise as now no longer all artists have this capacity. Since you're privy to this, you could count on that due to the fact your paintings is ideal it has correct ability to be sold. True, however allow us to remember all elements that want to be taken under consideration a step at a time.

1. You can be a superb artist, however in case your paintings does now no longer get observed and appreciated, it's far of no actual benefit. It is vital consequently that your paintings receives observed (through most exposure) and the manner to do that is get your call established.

This calls for which you touch the proper reassets and technique artists who've been thru the 'equal' mastering curve because it have been to attain the course of prosperity. You need to think about opposition that can exist in your preferred field. You have to put together a terrific foundation – this may be completed the usage of the records in the pages of this ebook.

2. Your paintings can be exceedingly lovely, however with out expertise the dynamics of the marketplace region your paintings might not blossom.

3. From your private angle your paintings might also additionally appear to have splendid cappotential. However, it's far applicable to understand the perspectives of the overall public – in different phrases your capacity buyers.

Do now no longer get into the rut that maximum do, "listening to what we need to hear" that is a kind of preconditioning that may convey untold misery.

4. You should check out different regions to expand your cappotential. Expand on problem category/theme, use of numerous unique varieties of media (e.g. acrylics, oils. Mixed media etc.), selecting the way to sell your paintings, you could even need to promote originals or reproduce prints possibly... The opportunities are endless, the query is how decided you're on your quest to be triumphant.

The psychology of achievement relies upon on wide variety of elements, however the one I agree with this is maximum critical is self-notion. Most humans in no way get the primary level of achievement due to the fact they lack this characteristic, that is critical. Such conditioning regularly stems out of your private reports, however the causative issue is surroundings, which has already been mentioned.

Though it is ideal to be careful approximately something which you do in existence, it's far similarly vital which you do now no longer get tangled into the technicalities of the 'process', however instead attention at the advantages and the closing praise that it yields.

Dedicate your aim to reaching fulfillment via way of means of enforcing the 5 cardinal phrases starting with the letter D on your fulfillment, specifically Devotion, Discrimination, Discipline, determination and Duty. There isn't anyt any damage in elevating questions concerning proposals that come your manner or maybe enterprise possibilities you propose pursuing. So lengthy as those questions come up with the money for all of the solutions and that making a decision to comply with thru thinking about all of the factors, then it's miles all nicely and correct.

However, whilst your questions defeat the very motive of your inquiry then it will become a 'vicious cycle'.

Why, what, wherein, while, who're phrases that we frequently use to envision facts approximately the whole lot in lifestyles which includes commercial enterprise ventures – accordingly giving upward push to questions.

The query with the phrase why is a need for it'll assist us draw an excellent end and assist us conquer doubts. The hassle with that is that in case you aren't clean approximately your aim(s), then the very query why you desire to even pursue the challenge turns into meaningless.

What you ought to remember are possibly lengthy-time period desires, blessings and the way your first step to wealth and achievement will allow you to experience more heights.

CHAPTER 3
The Inevitable Mistakes

As humans we're very restless – we frequently grow to be beaten with pleasure, fulfillment or gratification. It is so very critical to preserve your calm all through such events, due to the fact exhilaration can result in troubles, of which one is over spending. That stated, it's also pretty essential to comprehend that fulfillment can also additionally simply 'knock' you returned, in that you can end up complacent and 'determine' now no longer to do a lot, due to the fact you 'have it all'. This is a horrible segment that you may ever probable get into, and one you should consciously be aware about in any respect times. However, the only factor which you have to watch out for is the ego complex – Never allow your ego emerge as an obstacle for your enterprise to reap wealth. The first-rate medicinal drug to keep away from ego is to preserve power. The power that has been generated and conserved, until it's miles directed into the proper channels, it is going to be catastrophic.

We have to manipulate our urges, and that is wherein the artwork of working towards stability in existence turns into an critical device on your fulfillment. Idle communicate is one unmarried issue that may wreck your preference to succeed. Remember, that human beings round you and the organization you've got got will decide your destiny fulfillment – you could waste treasured time, however the ones round you'll make it even worse, they'll make a contribution to general wastage of your very own time. Thus because the pronouncing goes, 'like draws like' must be the maxim, and chiefly use your not unusualplace feel all of the time, and handiest do this which produces high-quality effects. Being systematic too will assist keep away from confusion and annoyances, that could each, have an destructive impact for your commercial enterprise assignment and desires. Do now no longer tackle board paintings which could set you lower back.

Try to assess the scenario, paying a lot significance on priorities – do now no longer procrastinate, do now no longer waste time and maximum of all do now no longer waste your valuable power. If you act thoughtfully then time can be controlled maximum efficiently. If phrases, deeds, mind and movements are right then existence might be true, and every second will convey fulfillment and 'time' taken to gain the coveted aim can be...nicely your wager is as true as mine. "Mind is the reason for bondage and freedom."

The Law of Success

Simply via way of means of expertise not unusualplace ideas, of which a few have already been mentioned above, it is easy to acquire achievement. A aware attempt must be made to offer appropriate reports for the thoughts. Nature has supplied guy with the entirety in big abundance – unluckily aleven though people have now no longer pretty found out this truth. You have to make up your thoughts to be a success. How are you able to try this successfully? How are you able to broaden will? Success comes with planning, dedication and religion no question. To verify this truth I endorse which you attempt the subsequent: Choose a few goal which you assume you can't accomplish, after which attempt with all of your strength and energy to do this one factor.

This can be something, from drawing a portrait to gaining knowledge of the way to use the computer. When you've got got completed fulfillment, cross directly to some thing larger and hold striving ahead exercise your willpower. Despite any set backs do now no longer be shaken in any respect, however derive energy out of your environment and mainly examine from like-minded humans who've sought to gain fulfillment courageously with out ever dropping hope. Remind yourselves of humans like Abraham Lincoln, Henry Ford, Mother Teresa and lots of greater who've executed the coveted position, due to their innate energy of religion and dynamic willpower. Remember, you can also reap the equal fulfillment.

This regulation may be carried out with the aid of using everybody and it does paintings. It is real that our mind and moves form our destiny and destiny. You have to be inclined to channel your skills and innate talents withinside the proper direction, so you can leap to new heights.

To recap on what has been stated hence far, permit me to remind you what it takes to be a success.

• Planning is vital and possibly the maximum vital step in your fulfillment.

• Prepare your self to extrade your views, conduct and your idea patterns.

• Only pursue duties which might be crucial. You have to divide your wishes out of your wants – there's a great line, so workout discrimination.

• Watch your private monetary scenario. Budget properly and decrease spending.

• Surround your self with humans with a nice personality and people who're a hit. Read books approximately human beings who've succeeded in lifestyles.

• Do now no longer faux to be who you aren't. Be your self and do now no longer display off.

• Expand your horizon and be enthusiastic and ambitious.

- It is ideal to boom your earnings however it's far even higher to spend money on belongings in order to make you wealthy.

- Prepare to paintings tough and make sacrifices.

Right moves enrich, reinforce and encourage us absolutely vitalizing our internal resources. Cultivation of such values and adhering to the proper values of residing will assist us develop and gain achievement. Such a regular regime and publicity can mold our individual and could assist redeem our decrease dispositions.

Time to Learn Who You Are

I might frown upon anybody who might even consider creating a comment, through announcing that fulfillment is best a wishful notion. We aren't born disasters – allow me get this factor straightened. We have all been a hit in our lives at a few degree or every other, and that is an plain truth. The following factors will honestly allow you to recognize who you truly are, and that may be a guarantee. Once you confirm your very own attributes, it turns into that lots less complicated to include beliefs in order to permit you to bounce to extra heights.

1. Are you usually enthusiastic and tremendous or the entire opposite?

2. Do you want to paintings tough and might you install that little little bit of more attempt in case you did what you like maximum?

3. Are you being all that you may be – you could need to research your strengths and weaknesses.

4. Are you content material together along with your gift state of affairs and/or circumstances? Upon answering those 3 very critical issues, you may decide your destiny. Remind yourselves

approximately the significance of field and corporation referred to in advance.

The subsequent factor I desire to spotlight is simplicity. Do now no longer unnecessarily create hardships withinside the manner of your work and the aim to fulfillment. By simplicity I imply, do now no longer complicate state of affairs, and do now no longer allow fulfillment get for your head – pompous mindset is but any other hassle which can convey you down. Be humble, assertive and righteous to your endeavors to succeed. A calm man or woman can attain truly something clearly thru the electricity of attention – that is a systematic primarily based totally reality. Research has surely proven that strategies like yoga, visualization, and rest can convey heightened awareness, thereby permitting the person to attain his most potential. By the electricity of attention and awareness, someone can do so which he/she has preferred.

The Need for Change

We are all too conscious that not anything ever stays everlasting in lifestyles, despite know-how one truth that existence itself is a continuum, what we've got did not comprehend is that our personal attitudes, conditioning and propensities stops us from incorporating modifications. One of the maximum tough matters to extrade is our nature (the indelible mind), mainly those who have left a mark (blueprint) on our psyche. We can be capable of alternate plenty of factors round us however the want to extrade our mind, attitudes and behavior which nearly absolutely have end up part of our self identification will become arduously tough a assignment.

As with all matters in existence time can heal whatever and the entirety – permit time that will help you develop in lifestyles and with out losing time attain your person dreams. How can we extrade our intellectual mindset? The solution may be very easy – once more there may be no mystery as such, neither is this hard a project to enforce. The number one solution lies withinside the phrase alternate itself. Initiating slow adjustments for your way of life will assist you attain your aim a good deal faster. I say that the solution is straightforward with appreciate to how we will result in advantageous modifications, due to the fact allow us to do not forget behavior for instance. Habits take time to take root, as we're all too conscious. Just as you 'research' your behavior with time you definitely start to unlearn them. Habits are very tough to get rid of at as soon as, and therefore you permit time to attend to your behavior. What has this were given to do with being satisfied and rich, I 'hear' you ask? Well, my buddies I would love to throw again the very equal query to you! Ask your self why you haven't been capable of development? Put into exercise what you've got got collected consequently far. Sit in a quiet nook and open your coronary heart out, and resolve this hassle – the solution to all you issues desirable or horrific lie inside you. The exactness of the hassle will no question vary, however the cause(s) for it are self-explanatory.

They stem from studies, surroundings and your concept patterns. Why is it that individual Y is capable of end smoking and but individual Z has an awful lot problems to cease the habit, aleven though each were smoking for ten years, and each smoke twenty cigarettes a day? The solution lies in what I actually have already mentioned above, and it's far our thoughts. The one issue that you'll should alternate for your lifestyles is your modern notion of who you're, what others consider you and in the end who you sincerely are? While you may extrade your mind, your surroundings and your enterprise strategies, what you may ought to comprehend is that you'll now no longer be capable of extrade the very Law of Nature – it's far perfect. Thus, we need to appreciate this and start to stick to its governing dynamics, with out violating it. How can nature have an effect on our fulfillment?

This is a legitimate query, however upon deep evaluation you'll recognize that we as humans are continuously breaking the rules, legal guidelines and lifestyles's everlasting methods day by day. Without digressing from the problem depend too a great deal, cautiously watch and note how the stunning rhythm of nature is pleasing its obligation each day with none discordance, and interruption. Likewise we've lots to examine from Nature. Deviation from fact results in utter dismay and failure, and breaking the Laws of Nature will carry despair – in brief the macrocosm and the microcosm are indifferent. The choices which you make for your existence will decide the final results of your destiny events. Always assume first of what you're approximately to do or intend doing, and through assignment this act how will it then have an effect on you. Do not act on impulse, however as a substitute stay calm, quiet and attempt to keep deep silence as lots as you may. It is in reality first rate what you could attain thru silence and introspection.

I do endorse which you adopt a shape of rest workout, inclusive of meditation or maybe yoga that will help you attain peace and achievement. Good judgment is a super indicator of know-how thru the expression of the electricity of mind through the discriminative faculty. If you've got got in reality identified your folly, then you definitely have to admit errors and awful behavior. If it annoys others or influences your fitness, conscience, monetary status, own circle of relatives, nicely-being and your peace of thoughts, you then definately should ask, 'How a lot higher off might I be with out it?' If you do now no longer gain from this – why even take it up or consider it.

CHAPTER 4

Understanding Failure

'Reason is the finest enemy that religion has.' This is a reality due to the fact each the believer and the non-believer are pretty probably to lodge to this announcement in help in their respective arguments. You have already been familiar to lifestyles's dualistic nature, and as such human cause will discover each 'pros' and cons' for each exact and horrific movement respectively. This is if you have to learn how to be guided through the internal voice of 'conscience'. The following stand up from this innate powerhouse, intuition, reality, peace, righteousness, love, nonviolence (in phrases, deeds, movements and mind) and strength of discrimination. These attributes have their life withinside the soul. This is the finest fact which you can't find the money for now no longer to know. Effort is proportional to grace, however I desire to feature that fulfillment is proportional to attempt most effective if you have discovered to realize the characteristics of love. Whatever you do installed all of your attempt and do anything you do with absolute love.

Those who're inclined to take dangers reap achievement. It is a acknowledged truth, that younger human beings are extra adaptable to modifications. As we age it will become a touch elaborate and more difficult to result in modifications and the capacity to conform to extensive ranging consolation zones. Before it will become too late, weed out the trouble early on – do now no longer permit it gnaw into your device. Like a plague take motion and do away with it out of your gadget at as soon as. The truth is that we're born perfect (I do now no longer imply this in a bodily experience of the phrase), however the rigors of time 'adulterates' this perfection, and consequently the countless opportunities that lie lurking inside us grow to be diffused.

However, what makes us advanced is that there's however one fantastic and covetable present that is ours all of the time, and that is our fantastic energy to discover, broaden and claim that we as humans have the ability to attain splendid if now no longer more heights – mendacity inside us is the limitless supply of strength this is pretty ours! "We are helpless sufferers of our very own goals and wants."

The Final Goal

Most human beings as I am positive you'll agree do the whole thing half-heartedly, and the motives(s) for this have all been covered. They do now no longer use their complete potential, particularly due to the fact they've now no longer understood the strength of the thoughts. Often we're drawn or pressured to do matters that convey sorrow. Temporary pleasures carry sorrow, and therefore majority folks thru worry or possibly even loss of self belief are 'forced' to throw withinside the white towel. This want now no longer be the case, due to the fact this ee-e book offers you the capacity to triumph over those hurdles, through turning in phrases so powerful that you may alternate your circumstances. It is excessive time which you watch the graphs of your thoughts very cautiously.

Upon introspection it's miles now time to weed out the dust and via the usage of the energy of discrimination distinguish that which offers you lasting happiness instead of sorrow. The backside line is you need to exercising manipulate over your mind. The following is protected to manual you in your adventure to wealth, fitness and happiness.

• Avoid living on all of the wrongs matters you've got got done.

• Repeating incorrect moves time and again end up behavior. Simply take care now no longer to copy the ones movements again.

• Do now no longer think about your self as a failure. Use screw ups as a way to obtaining fulfillment – do not longer surrender till you attain your preferred purpose.

• You will ought to erase the grooves of terrible behavior which you have created via way of means of growing exact conduct. If you're lazy determine to come to be definitely energetic and assertive – set your self duties or dreams and ensure you acquire them.

The truth that we face up to alternate indicates that we've our very own 'consolation zones' and that is a end result of our mind. Why is it that we face up to extrade – the easy solution to this query is worry of alternate.

A alternate manner that we ought to allow cross of that which we 'sense' is 'proper' for us.

The query then stays to be requested is what's proper for you? This is a tough one, and the solution is that till we aren't absolutely content material inside ourselves then even a millionaire who goals a further million is a beggar. How a lot of us are content material?

We are looking for immediately outcomes, and while we do now no longer 'see' outcomes we end up despondent and finally surrender. It is my notion that while you choice a component for the proper motives then not anything will ever prevent you from obtaining it – that is the everlasting regulation.

Paving Your Path to Success

I wrote this ee-e book with handiest one purpose in thoughts and this is that will help you apprehend and in the long run assist you recognise the Power of the Mind. What you'll quickly discover is a chain of steps that you need to comply with very strictly to examine your deep-seated preference. These steps aren't huge obligations, however easy pointers to get you started.

1. Believe in your self, and the energy of affirmations. Successful humans turn out to be a success thru steady use in their willpower. Do not be scared of mishaps withinside the preliminary stages. Transform screw ups into fulfillment thru expertise, energy and religion.

2. Believe withinside the philosophy of 'easy dwelling and excessive thinking'.

3. Do not maintain some thing in opposition to every person. Strive to triumph over your beyond grievances and flow on. Try to forgive everybody 'harm in no way assist ever'.

4. Honesty is the golden rule. Observe silence, meditate and get rid of all bad inclinations out of your machine (i.e. jealousy, ego, hatred, worry and so on). Stick to the subsequent ideas, love, fact, righteousness, peace and non-violence (you have not to even injure everyone thru your speech, moves and mind). With absolute willpower, it's far applicable that to collect achievement you companion with human beings who've already attained it.

To respect the cause of this e book, it turns into vitally critical to scrutinize the subsequent factors. It will make extra feel to you presently why fulfillment or failure relies upon on the way you outline your self:

IMAGE: The higher you sense approximately your self-picture the much more likely you'll succeed. Image does now no longer always suggest looks; it additionally has a deeper that means and connotes reflection. The picture that you could have approximately your self is much more likely to stem from what you 'suppose' approximately your self. The inner surroundings that I even have mentioned in advance can play a critical function in figuring out your very last intention.

EMOTIONS: It is plain that our mind and feelings, that are diffused, have exceptional affect in our lives. The excellent manner to counteract those diffused forces is to exercising silence in the course of meditation and rest exercises.

It is recommended to absorb a shape of workout to maintain your thoughts definitely lively. Of route the second one gain is fitness. Healthy frame serves as a great 'vehicle' to do nicely.

Every man or woman seeks happiness in existence. Now the very happiness we are searching for turns into a pleasure as soon as found. This pleasure can surmount to 'bliss' absolutely through incorporating.

LOVE. You have to percentage love in what you do and also you should love what you accomplish each day on your existence. In the silence of the night, introspect and discover ways to enhance your existence (in phrases, deeds, mind and movements) and thank the ideal time-honored power.

Together with what has been stated above, proper communique skills, interplay and excellent courting is the manner ahead – that is in the long run the essence of first-rate virtues and person in order to make you a hit. Develop a harmonious personality, and keep in mind what become stated on the begin, usually use loving phrases – phrases can convey peace or begin a international war. Conditioning your thoughts successfully will assist you to attain the rewards. It is excellent exercise to scrutinize your every day mind simply previous to bedtime, and log this on your development e book. Set desires and goals day by day and paintings at it till you attain them.

Time is the maximum valuable asset in lifestyles, use it wisely – time wasted is lifestyles wasted. When you make a decision to attain fulfillment for your existence, make certain you do now no longer have conflicting mind. If you discover ways to consciously manipulate and therefore enforce the inexhaustible powers inside you, you may accomplish tons extra. Language is not anything however the expression of mind and studies. Communication performs a important position for your standard achievement, a good deal much less your everyday dwelling. Through the energy of knowledge, you may gain precise dreams, due to the fact the name of the game of our energy is in our knowledge. When you've got got an concept this is potential it's miles vital to recognition on it hundred percentage.

Never inform the arena approximately it – there's no want for such 'display'. Ponder over it and broaden it into a 'product' that has a valid base. Without a company basis an edifice has no danger to stand.

The Law of Prosperity

There isn't anyt any damage to choice fulfillment and all of the different proper matters in lifestyles, however relaxation assured, preference which results in the nagging feeling of lack or incompleteness may be dangerous. If for any cause choice results in sleepless nights and frustration - it's time to STOP anything is it which you are doing. Contentment is the actual unmarried aspect of maintaining your abundance. A egocentric preference results in utter failure! Spiritual regulation could be very effective indeed. That stated, you need to enterprise to comply with the subsequent concepts every day to your lifestyles. Always be excellent to all round you, do now no longer be treacherous and deceitful. Beware of the ego and be actual and sincere.

Thoughtfulness is exceedingly critical, so usually remind your self of folks who might not be so lucky, and make bigger your assisting hand as plenty as you probable can to folks who deserve it. Training your thoughts to perform wonderful heights isn't a tough project. In your spare time, do not waste your strength; as a substitute spend time considering at the electricity of your innate being. Meditate every day and visualize your fulfillment and your dreams. My pals, the strength of the thoughts is in reality awesome, the reality is that we do now no longer even use 10 percentage of it in our day by day lives – now primarily based totally in this clinical expertise simply consider what you may gain in case you had been to apply the final ninety percentage.

Just as you take pleasure in meals while you bite it and flavor it – carry out every and each act with a experience of gratitude and do it willingly and most significantly happily.

Do NOT observe each little impulse blindly, learn how to mirror and distinguish among what's brief and fleeting and what's lasting, what's critical and what's non vital, among what's attractive and what's unworthy. Self-conquest will supply us that which we're seeking. It needs to be harassed that stability is likewise an vital aspect for your quest for achievement and wealth. You should allocate time for your self and your own circle of relatives or the cherished one's. A everlasting happiness have to be impartial of a converting surroundings.

converting environment.

Never end up a workaholic or a 'wealthpreneur' freak for your quest to fulfillment, lest it damages your relationship, a great deal much less your tries to simply reach existence. Never deviate from the course of righteousness or the Law of Nature. It is amazing amusing certainly to witness fulfillment and wealth, and the pleasure that wells up is past perception no doubt. However, if happiness, pleasure and fulfillment all come immediately on the price of your health, then I am afraid it's far all a horrible waste. The manner to being rich, is through the employment of the subsequent virtues that's our actual actual nature, and it's miles to be observed now no longer simply in humans however the whole thing round you: Truth, righteousness, peace, love and non violence. Ask your self, that if all fellow people practice those attributes consistently – the sector and its population might prosper.

We have to technique all our paintings (together with problems) or obligations with focused electricity and hence execute it with absolute perfection. Endeavor to do all of the things (little or but small a obligation or activity this can be) in an extremely good manner. Perform all of your paintings and responsibility with LOVE and enthusiasm, and watch the results. Never try some thing 1/2 of heatedly; you may now no longer development in lifestyles.

Power of Words

Power of phrases will have a completely robust effect on our minds and in our lives. Before I continue, I would love you to cogitate on the subsequent question, may want to a person continue to be silent in any respect instances. Not letting all and sundry realize what's internal his/her coronary heart and thoughts for the mere purpose of now no longer being verbally or emotionally expressive? Yet I can say with fact that every and each one folks are silent talkers. We communicate to ourselves in lots of approaches and situations, a few instances we harm ourselves and but at different instances, silent speaking brings a brilliant smile to our faces!

Communication is consequently very essential in existence. Words are effective and relying how they're spoken, they are able to affect our daily notion processes, movements, conduct and our outlook toward lifestyles as a whole. Of direction relying on how they're used the impact phrases could have is pretty incredible, they may be used to persuade, inform, harm, ease ache or maybe begin a war! Words spoken with incredible feelings have the energy to convey modifications that could accelerate the frame's restoration process! This good sized energy is withinside the which means of the phrases, what they suggest to the individual that hears them. Far extra than easy communique, truth, falsehood and the countless sun sunglasses among them, phrases have the electricity to control different human beings's wondering and conduct. It is our interpretation of phrases this is the genuine reason of our emotional reactions. Words spoken softly, unselfishly, innocently and with absolute love are those that get lodged indelibly in our being from whence they produce their overwhelming soul stirring impact. Thus it's so vital to apply phrases selectively and accurately at any given time and situation. Modern technology is starting to respect the effective impact phrases may have on our our bodies while they're used withinside the shape of prayers or maybe affirmations. Did that thru aware effort, we ought to create a completely robust strength of will in ourselves?

Affirmation for fulfillment:

I will pursue relentlessly, as it's far my birthright to be successful. I am effective and I shall acquire what I want on the time I want. I am destined to acquire the culmination of my moves and I will percentage my pleasure in fulfillment with all I understand.

Benefits of Affirmations

- Self-esteem and a fine outlook

- Helps you reap dreams and targets

- Improve you reminiscence and skills

- Helps to create an internal self-notion (self-control, self belief and character)

- It allow you to evolve spiritually

Words spoken softly lightly and lovingly could be appealing and acquire immediate admiration. Wealth is in itself a phrase, and with the aid of using itself it does now no longer imply whatever.

The one unmarried factor, which offers the phrase wealth, the which means is the mind. The wealth of statistics is nowhere to be observed, however it's miles inside us in any respect instances. Intellect is cultivated via common sense, and the primary factor is that dry good judgment and philosophy can regularly show counter productive. Thus, it's far important to talk effectively, due to the fact in pursuit of wealth, you may want to promote your self your commercial enterprise or your agency through communique (phrases). However, verbal exchange on its very own will now no longer reciprocate your fulfillment.

The Power of Unconditional Love

It appears to me that humans have forgotten the actual price, which means and definition of the phrase love. You may also exclaim and say what has love were given to do with wealth! It is obviously hard to outline proper love, allow me explain, say you need to discover ways to swim, you examine books approximately the artwork of turning into an awesome swimmer, however till you do now no longer leap into the swimming pool beneathneath guidance, the real which means of swimming does now no longer have any actual price or which means. You will ought to flavor the fruit to recognise its actual flavor, because the announcing goes. Selfish love rooted in dreams which are in no manner harmonious is the maximum damaging, and in case you end up 'immersed' in obtaining your desires through deception, calumny and towards all of the noble and moral concepts than you would possibly as nicely positioned this ee-e book away. Those who recognize love stay in concord and it's far herbal that those people will appeal to what they've willed to gain. The best electricity of appeal in each feel of the phrase be it a relationship, commercial enterprise and friendship is love.

As a budding entrepreneur, take into account that the appealing energy of affection is incredible – you ought to exercise compassion, and watch your self develop and watch your task thrive. Upon attaining any shape of fulfillment in existence it turns into pertinent that regardless of what happens, you do now no longer pressure your fulfillment on anybody – keep away from egoism, satisfaction and do now no longer impose your electricity on everyone – it is incorrect to do so. It is vital that with the aid of using getting rich, you do now no longer abuse your newly acquired 'electricity'. When energy is used as it should be realize which you have carried out glory.

Conclusion

This ebook is written with the view to permit you to determine the innate latent powers that lie dormant inside every and all of us folks. Opportunity seekers can't sincerely find the money for to 'selected and pick', however as an alternative they have to learn how to capitalize on each little bit of danger this is afforded to them. As a seeker avail your self to possibilities which have the capability to turn out to be quintessential gateway to achievement – it's far all approximately taking calculated, controlled, measured and an knowledgeable risk. Wealthy people have created their personal profession due to the fact they're actual believers of fulfillment.

These are those who can't prevent till they gain achievement. They end up rebellious opponents most effective to earn their unflinching goal – they may be disciplined warriors wielding their guns of truth, honesty, sincerity, compassion, determination, energy, standards, righteousness, wisdom, faith, self-perception, creativity, fortitude and prowess to attain heights par excellence. Life capabilities strictly in line with the natures incorrigible laws. The motive for that is to set up efficiency, and withinside the ambit of law, the rational mind in guy may be evolved to a more efficiency.

You are rich already, but because of the lack of expertise your effective innate qualities, those attributes mendacity in abundance have now no longer observed the dynamism to explicit and manifest. Finally do now no longer take lifestyles too seriously. Life is a adventure made feasible for us all, and if we're inclined to provide ourselves the possibility to develop, then lifestyles may be so first-rate an experience. It is maximum entertaining, specially while one follows its governing ideas religiously.

ABOUT THE AUTHOR

Chindu Aneke is from a good family in African, He studied in one of the best Universities in African, He later obtained his master degree in library science in the US. He currently live in US.